Buffy's House of Mirrors

ALSO BY KIM MALINOWSKI

Home
Phantom Reflection
Death: A Love Story
The Fool's Journey (forthcoming)
We Could Be Lovers (forthcoming)

Buffy's House of Mirrors

kim malinowski

artwork by gabby gilliam

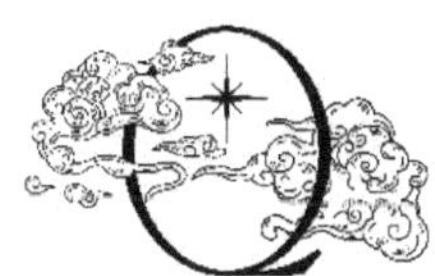

Q an Imprint of Querencia Press
Chicago, IL

Q AN IMPRINT OF QUERENCIA PRESS

ISBN 978 1 959118 70 1

www.querenciapress.com

First Published in 2023

Querencia Press
Chicago IL

Printed & Bound in the United States of America

For all those slaying their demons

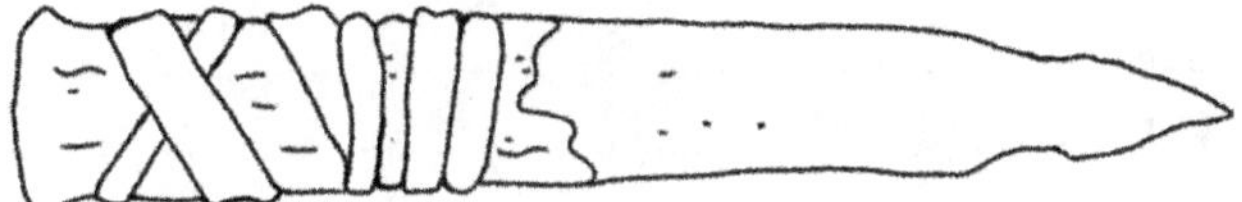

Trigger Warnings for

Eating Disorders & Body Image

CONTENTS

Into the House of Mirrors

Funhouse mirrors, zany shapes, sizes,
gawdy bobbles and bits,
flash of lights,
round and round
and who am I to stake?
The woman in the left two mirrors
lost her soul,
her brow bumped,
eyes dark, familiar, hurt.
Sucked by love and not love,
strangled soul fled without
vampire kiss.
A million things mean love,
a million things mean sacrifice,
a million things tell her she is undeserving,
mean, selfish, too large, too thin,
too dumb, teeth too yellow,
hair not yellow enough,
and that's not the demon in the reflection,
that is the one holding the stake.

"Give me something to sing about"

I don't have background dancers
not in sync with any damn beat.
No dizzying snare or slam of guitar rift
just splintered stake in my heart
and the open space you left on repeat.
No demon winding out my secrets with
snazzy syncopation and pizazz
no rewinding episodes to explain
incomplete character arcs about to explode
to every damn character's demise.
All that sappy hope, the kumbayayas,
all my wounds untreated
none stitched up tight.
Can't even riff myself into intoxicating burn.
Spike doesn't stop my frenetic dance to the death
and his eyes don't meet mine and croon
living will ease the pain, the suffering
is part of life. A necessary part, sure asshole.
And no matter how hot he is—
Buffy has dibs, and I have to perform my own triage
before the next take. Extract the stake that didn't miss, just
shattered, because the slayer didn't equip
himself for battle-hardened hearts.
So now with tweezer and needle, a shot of Writer's Tears,
I tend to the damage. Each splinter, each molecule,
because every vampire knows atomic and molecular
structure is the difference between a clean wound
and one that festers for centuries.

I hear the deep timber of my slayer's voice
shards zing out into ink
cacophony of treble clef and the hope for demon
duet with background accompaniment.
I'd take a viola and a trombone or two
in some waltz to demise under a Capricorn
sky and a pilgrimage past pain.
Spike and Buffy could have their fling.
I could have whatever tatters remain of my not-
fling that lasts centuries or seconds.
And his eyes are cold and soft and rigid and steel
my mouth prepares to sing to the demon's spell
maybe this time, I could get a dance number.
He smiles, a not Spike smile,
and I sigh a not Buffy sigh.
No one can tell us how to live being us.
My heart stops, waiting for the next stake.

First Published with Writers from Scars Publications

Lure

In one mirror there is a field of sunflowers,
the demon tan, smiling, alone.
She is bobbing around, taking silly photos,
posing as if she could know happiness.
Pretending.
          When did the demon bite me?
When I cantered to the food stand,
I had crisp ten dollar bills
and choice.
Mirrored truth.
          I did not buy food.
Oh, this mirror is silken,
polished with my broken promises.
          No, I did not buy food.
The demon traced my neck with fingers,
savored a last bit of sunlight.
Lemonade made in front of me,
lemon squeezed by metal, juice sliding
into cup. The first time I wanted taste
after so long.
This is where I should have gotten
back my soul but didn't.
A mix of sugar grit and lemon pulp
rolled in my mouth all day.
Losing my soul—or never getting one—
was worth it.
Thirst never quenched.
          Who needs food when there is tart,
                    sweet memory?

Triggered Selflove

Pretty, pretty, perfect
little demon! Spike
wouldn't love me,
wouldn't place finger on cheek,
or hand on waist,
sit by me in grief.
Wouldn't bite her,
or turn me,
or love me or love
her
and the one I loved
did not care about my demon.
Gentle with me
could not kill her or
love me
when I could not love
either.

Deserted Demon

It could be Sunnydale
with hands held out
holding darkness.
Mine clings,
sighs deep-bite into
heart. Lost. Always
on time for some ghoulish
location, some freak
out staccato phone
call to stranger that
my minutes compel
me to hold out my
phone.
Such talk
ends. My demon
cries and rips,
must be slain
and only I can
hold the stake.

Revealing Melee

Love. That annoying, reverberating word.
The bile when selflove is uttered. First need
that self-refrain.
I choke on the syllables, want peace,
not self-fucking-love.
Want back to tombstone
wait for stake,
pyre,

judgement.
Instead, bouncing reflections
mock me,
reflect all I am,
all I couldn't be.
How not-Buffy I am.
How not slayer.
How not vampire.
How not demon.
How I don't know my favorite color.
How I don't know my favorite style of shirt.
I don't want to know if I could fall to another dimension.
I would bring my wounds and my honey,
like baggage and carry my demons to paradise.

Caprice

The next mirror glows amber.
Smoky haze.
I smile, grit my teeth into it,
forced and sad
and loved
and I could not
would not
save myself.
Not in this funhouse,
not in magic reflection,
not in my fakeness.
My hair pinned and braided,
ready for ballroom,
my hair tangled, wild, ready for forest dance.
Would I kill for that illusive word to fill me?
At least once in my long and longer life?
Would I kill for its fierce, tongue, fangs?
Taste slayer, the mint of lips, the balm,
sliding on me as they brushed?
As she bruised?
Overripe plum?
I did not sing on leather jacket,
had no bondage boots,
impractical shoes disintegrated.
My slayer waited.
I was myself.

Plain, ruddy, marked
for pining away
or not loving at all.
My veins bitter.
My not-self pliable
with Buffy's super strength
and sharpened-teeth, my slayer lips
but in the mirror
or on the cool cracking side?

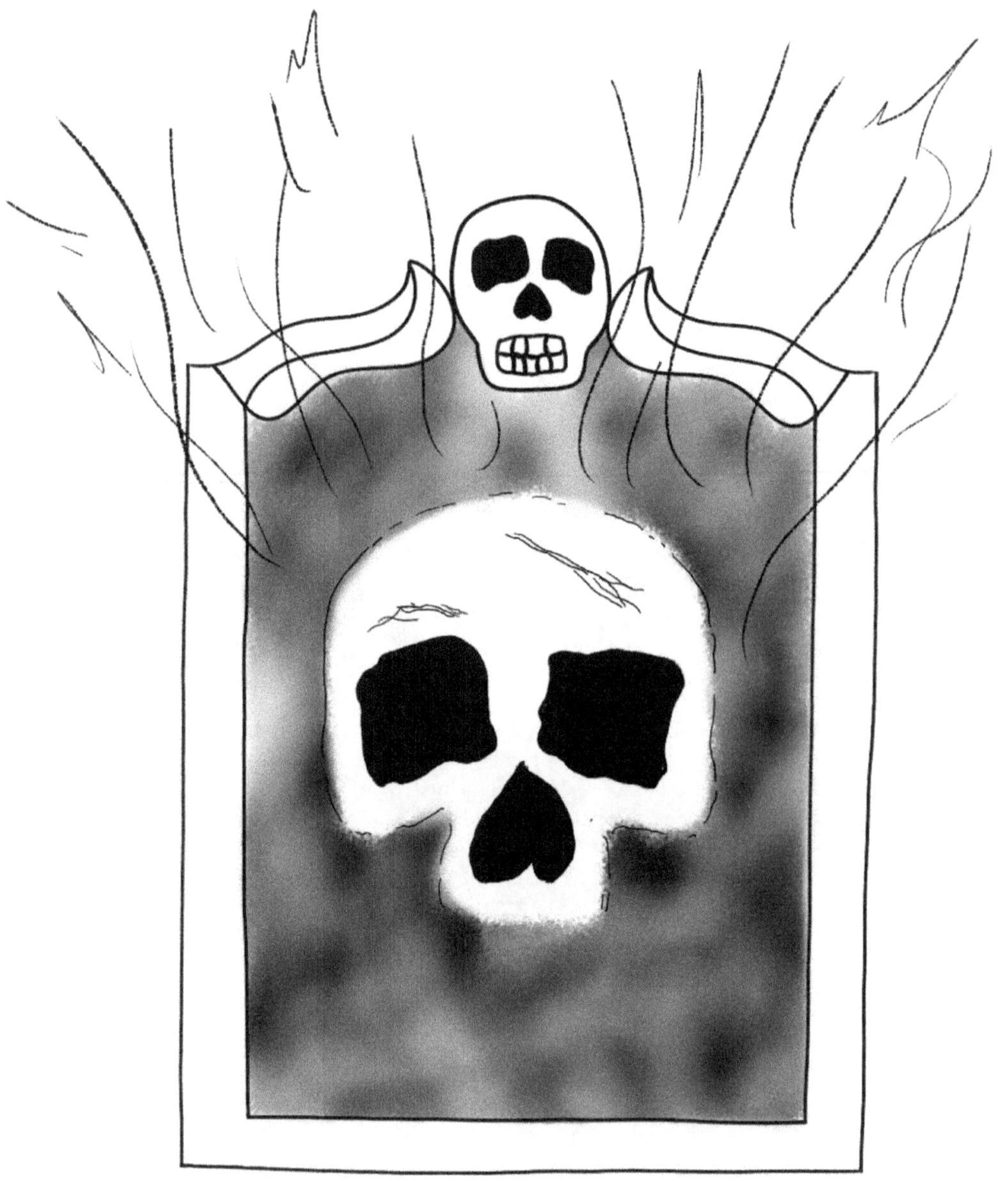

Some Fucking Advice Needed

Spike, why don't you tell him to save me?
Sing some fucking ode and grab his arm
hold a knife to his neck and ask if he wants
me to live or die or sing or waltz my way into ash?
Why does he not love me that way?
Why doesn't he say?
He takes my hand and keeps me from danger.
Protection without love? Protection with duty?
And yet—he does not want to lead me on—
as if I didn't question each action.
Spike—Buffy smacked you around so much—
is that what got your attention? What won
your dead heart? The pangs of my heart not
beating is why a stake looks so good—either into
his heart or mine. Or why-oh-why. And the song
plays, and the fires burn. Is he coming for me?
Or am I dancing stag?

Blurry Secrets

I could pretend this dimension forever.
Watch my not-afraid body.
Waist thick, proud.
Slayer shirt, belly button winking.
My swagger, and guile,
touch of fragility not to lose myself.
To tell the world I am enough.
I am enough.
To hear them whisper back.
You are enough.

Scattered Reflection

The mirror shatters.
Shards, shards, everywhere
but not enough to splinter his heart.
The girl in the mirror should be blonde.
Should have kickass bondage boots
and leather jacket of doom
and that's not me
anymore.
Boots disintegrate with time
and even if I freeze frame my image
I would find his apathy
in the woman's smile, in her hips,
her crow haunted eyes.
I pick up an edge of mirror
and the boot that smashed it.
The boot isn't mine.

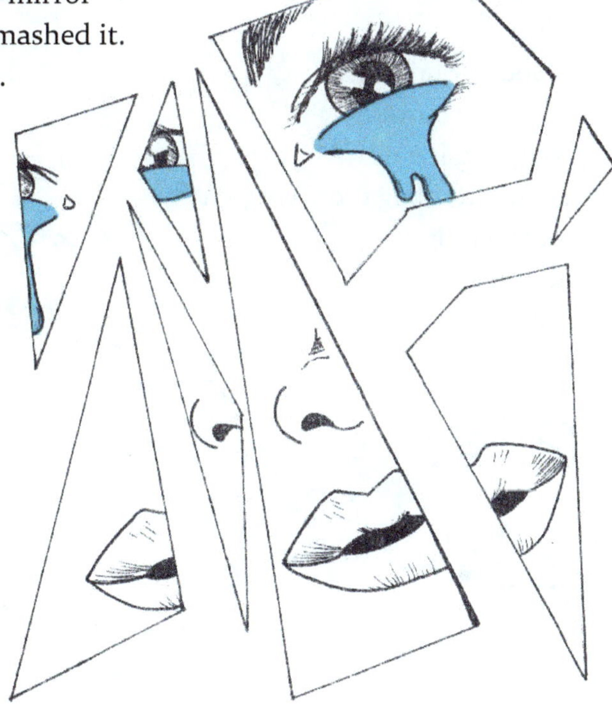

Trapeze Inside

I jump up. Shattered mirror
fragments tinkle happy.
I stand tall.
Thick hips.
Thick thighs.
Thick need.
She, It, clutches my throat,
grips my air away.
My demon trapped,
claws out.
Soul chewed,
spit out.
Only my fangs
satisfy
hush,
bloodlust lullaby.
I was the burden
weighing me down.
I could not beg cross rhythm
and spinning
accompaniments
a slayer
to save me.

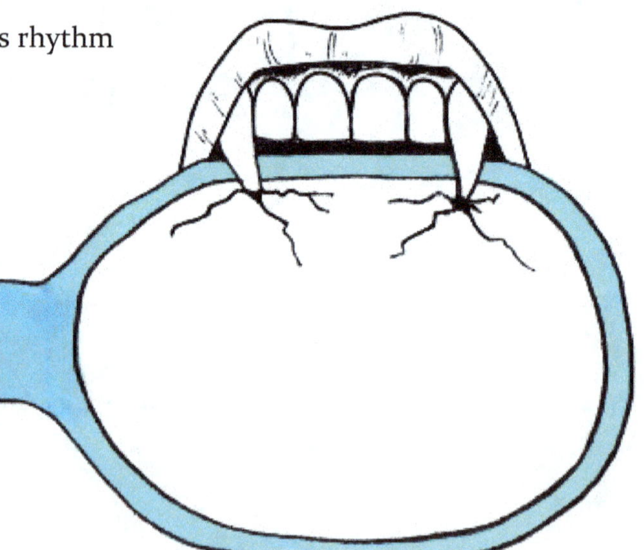

Coquette Covet

I've never been in Heaven.
Never had that bliss thing.
My heart peeled open
crushed by heels
stilettoed hard.
If you loved me—
would there be bliss?
Love twisted,
chest tearing.
If love feels like being ripped
from Heaven—why want it?
Crush too much weight.
Wait to sing refrain
lost love, lost world,
or the curtain call kiss.

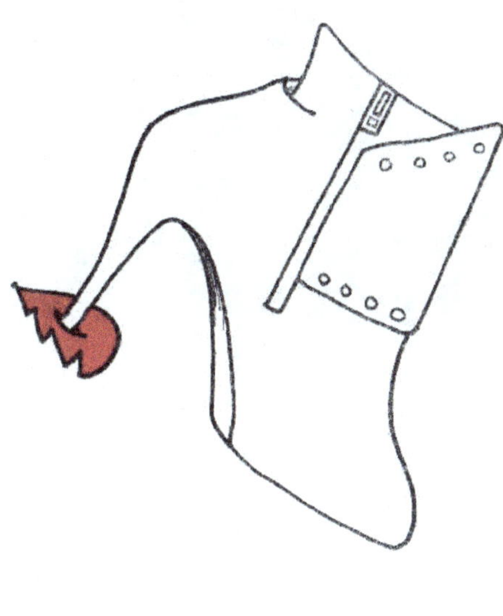

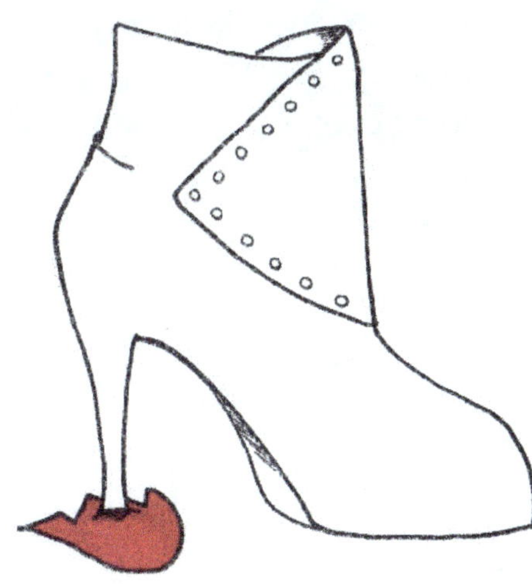

Let Me Rest in Peace

Golden Shovel Medley Riff on Terrance Hayes

Let me swallow back bile—ask
me for everything then the
rest is up to you
in your fragile
peace.

Pretend you've
not not-loved me, got
scared of me, a
sopping mess of willing,
reflecting your slave.

'cause I can be whoever I need
being something just for you
with soul or without
you don't even know my
touches,
don't even
know
me.

Interior Interrogation

I drop the boot.
Drop the broken glass,
hand already bloody.
Move to next sentient
mirror set before me.
I'm still alone.
Wear practical shoes.
Practice practical witchcraft.
I act simple, supple,
but am dark with a spell.
I step up.
Who am I?
My not-Buffy breasts.
My not-Willow lips.
Not Angel screaming into Angel-ous bliss
for me.
Who am I now?

Missing A Reflection

I look deep, deep,
deep into that mirror
expect plunge
as if my reflection
portals me in
allows me a place
at the table for two
set for one and a book.
Pit of stomach all thud.
No cure but living ditty,
playing percussion in belly.

I am alone. Not blessedly
alone as promised
by scarred walls, scary mirrors,
too bright lights, kilowatt colors.
Small, I am too much
Large, too much
muchness.

Everyone leaves me.
There is no reflection.
Am I vampire
or erasure?

Choice Chance Tango

What should I choose?
What could I choose?
Slayer, vampire, unclassified demon?
Choice to live.
Choice to live forever.
Like this.
I could have friendly gang,
could stake others' demons
over and over never ripping out
my own betrayal.
Heartbeat with thump, thump
palm slick,
squeezing,
too weak, too strong,
to slay myself.
The vampire sizzles to my kisses,
my heart likes it
as I lock it into place.
I am meant to end him.
He holds my hand.
The stake drops.
Echoes, colors flashing.
Even the mirror reverberates.
Failure. Failure. Failure.

I touch the glass barrier,
watching curtain close kiss.
Who am I to think
there ever was a choice?

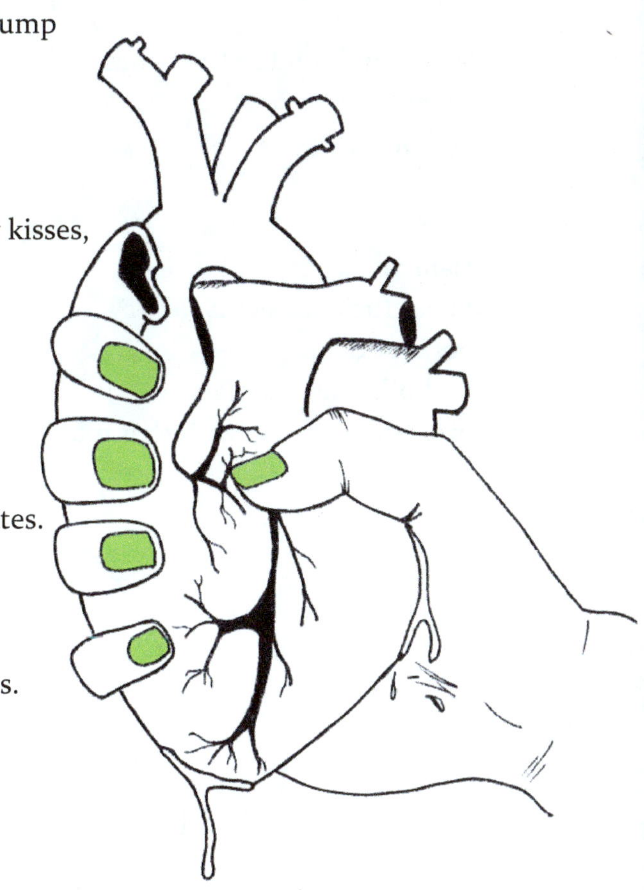

Combat Circus

Step right up.
Step right up.
I take off my shoe.
Heavy, clunky, perfect.
I don't like her either.

I slam

      that shoe

           like a railroad spike.

Damn, I'm proud as that woman's
brunette waves
and honest eyes
crack.

I slam and slam
not as efficient as that slayer
boot, but damn,
that hollow ass woman
never had a chance with that man.

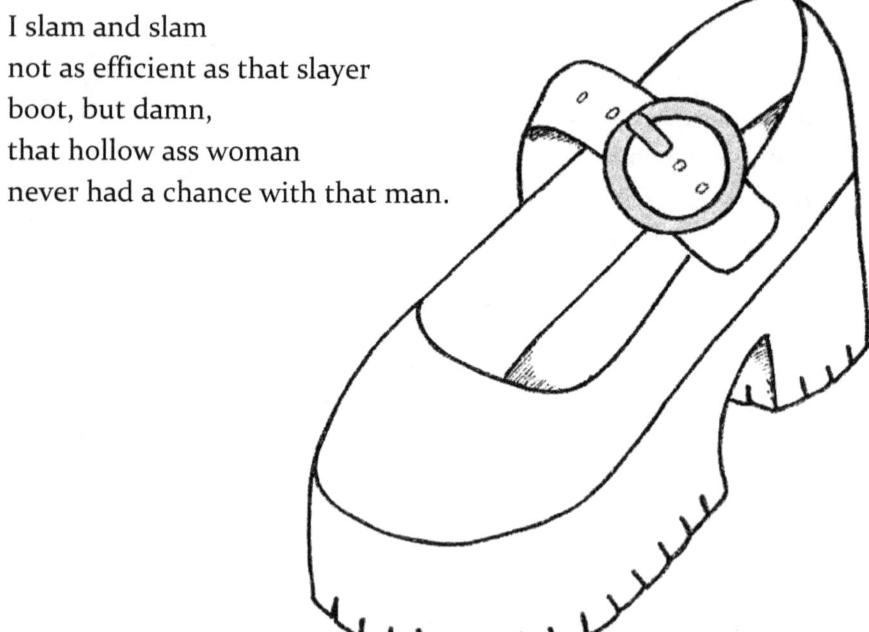

Heartbreak without a Stake

He chooses duty.
Of course.
Because all vampires
have to heroically sacrifice.
When is it time for me
not to be the sacrifice?
I can be the hero.
The mirror shrieks duty.
But sacrificing or sacrificed,
we are still damned dust.

Next Bloodlust . Kind Sir or Sire?

I stumble to the next mirror,
cracking forehead to reflection.
Dull thud reverberating sting through brow.
Who am I?
Who am I?
I cannot say.
I have only been told.

What if I was asked?
What do you want to be?

What if I could utter,
tongue not glued to tonsils?

What would I choose?

I cannot stop staring at my eyes.
Not even my bloody wound
panics me like my eyes.

Are they fierce? Defiant?

I have on denim, ripped t-shirt,
blood red lipstick, courage,
and like that I am in love.
Even if he comes behind me,
eyes glowing,
forehead bumped,

I am nobody.

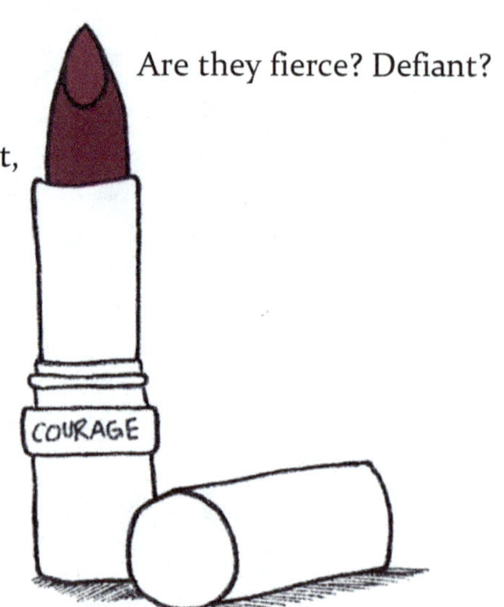

He will drink.
       I am so thirsty.
              He does not strike.
Dabs forehead.

Only vampire in this mirror.

He is a can't.
       Can't. Have. Him.
He is barred, closed off,
even as he gentles
me.

He could make me anyone he wants.
Could lead me to his desired mirror.
No makeup.
Full lip and shadow.
He stands up.
Walks through the glass.
Another place I cannot go.
My hand smacks.
I reach for his back.

No.
Not for me.

"I need something to sing about"

not the numbness in shoulders
weak muscles
tight smile
racoon eyes
fear
oh, love where are you? rag tag tonic
needed hand on shoulder
sing to collapse
ruin
didn't you know
that life wouldn't just go on
when you crawled into dungeon
and left me for dead?
I have a damn lot to sing about
it just isn't you.
That's just not enough.

Fractured History

The next mirror, ornate,
More mirror, mirror on the wall,
flashes my fangs, wicked ballgown,
long gloves slender, dapper.
I could collapse in wonder.
Corset frames breast heavenward.
I could be this demon.
Could whisper down some handkerchief.
Could be playful, tickle,
let someone unpin my hair,
chestnut.
I could be happy without peroxide hair.
Could let curls fall or frame
or cut lock by lock
some violent game of he loves me,
he loves me not.
Some hairbrush gliding through hair
one hundred times,
I love me. I love me not.

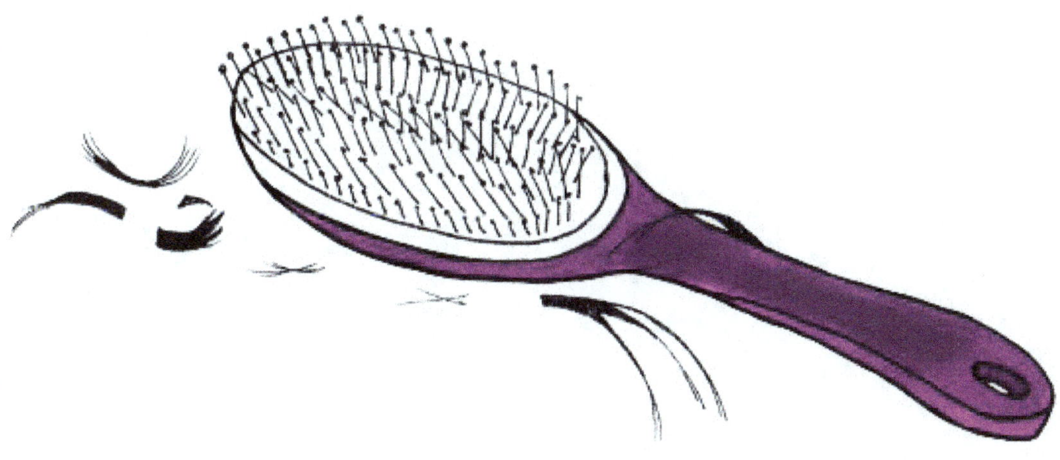

Crumbled Collapse

I leave the mirror whole.
Lump beside it.
Trace dried blood on fist.
Am I doomed forever?
The big forever-forever?
My mousy brown is already
slipping into white
complexion ruddy,
scared.
Donations and languid language
would sustain.
No patron cares about poetry
and rusty eyes
even if tongue dazzles into cavernous
geode display.
Hold only so long
before the shard
slices deep.

Hold No One

Shadow covers scene.
Gloves are gone.
Left are my rough,
bloody knuckles.
Pretend is a spell
that no one wants
to give away.
Just slay dancing,
just slip into cavernous dream.
Beg any deity,
and holy or unholy one
to let them stay.
Is heaven ripped away dream?
Can no one hold one safe
from bloody?
Teach to protect themselves?
To know their want and have no guilt?
I hear the demon's song.
Can no one buy dinner,
slide book into pocket,
let me follow from shadow
into warm hands?

Blatant Blister

I want to peel layers
of anxiety like sunburned skin.
Want to burn haunted itch.
Bring me fire.
I'll dowse myself in kerosine.
No need for demon to teach
me bad dance moves.
My nails dig into my flesh.
Where do I go from here?
Prescriptions twist me into pretzel,
antidote vampire bite.
I dare to grip Buffy's flame.
Let it freeze me into solid ache.
Unresolved tension when love
doesn't matter and want
makes us flame.

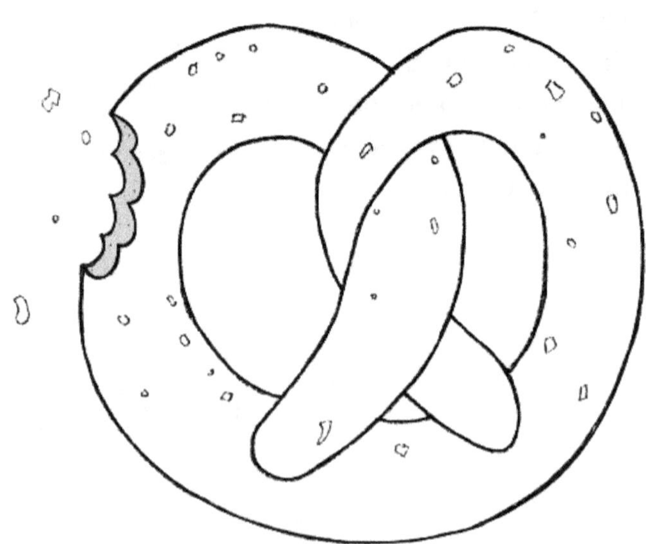

Barefoot Walk

Can I save the day?
Walk barefoot
with my own naïve outfit?
They sit by,
a funhouse mirror enlarges
breast and hips,
warps butt, thighs,
I know this is not me.
I am skirt and bare feet.
I am long hair and sunshine.

The demon can end it
in song.
Can scream in, impale myself,
or bite it into his heart.

Sophisticated Grace

In this mirror
I roll leg elegant
fall back into hard hands
eyes drift to doll face.
Struggle into another
man's arms.
Dance into capture
as I winter to fall
into love
or beg to get out of it.
I wear his talisman.
Branded.
No slayer needs to save me.
I will cavort with my shadows,
my brand will scar,
and I will be my own queen.

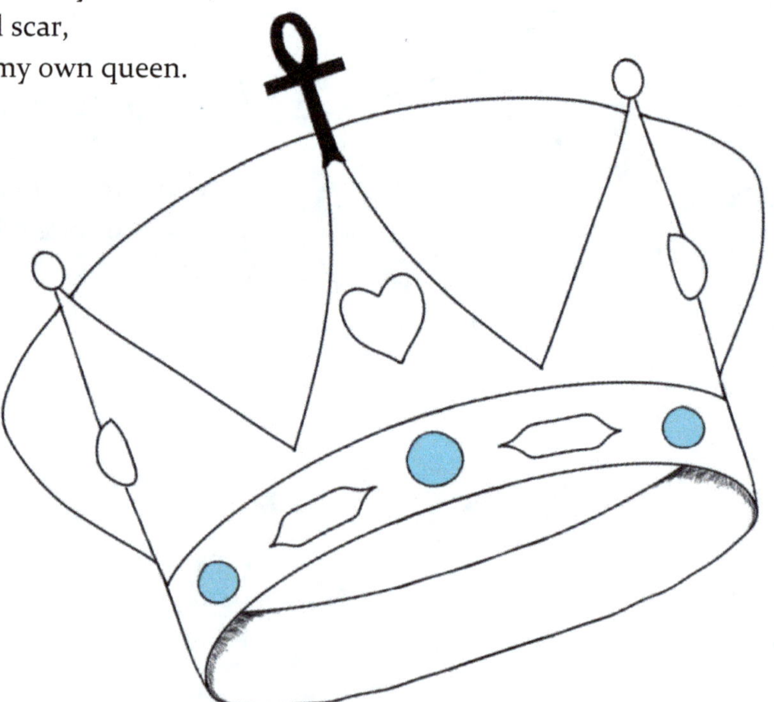

Pain IS Living

That burn in my cheeks is living.
The tube I apply to my lips is a tool.
A tool to trick my self-worth.
No. Love is better balm than red,
heat and self-hatred follow both.
I cannot wait.
It doesn't work like that.
You have to dance.
Even if you burn.
Dance to live.

"I died so many years ago but you can make me feel like it isn t so"

Golden Shovel after Terrance Hayes

Life isn't walking through a damn park, I
can't lay beneath a willow unless I've died.
You can't even save my shadow,
try, if you must. You, making too many
hollow gestures. You've played my song for years.
I sing umbra now, not long ago
my answers found your lips, but
your answers, I already buried deep in you.
You spill 'hope'—empty word to
hack at the void in my depths, make
violin lungs twang banjos and me—
I sweep pieces of exploding feel-
ings. You stake me hard like
lovesick demon. Accidental words break me it
hurts too much when ignored and yes, isn't
my heart too tender? You seem to know so.

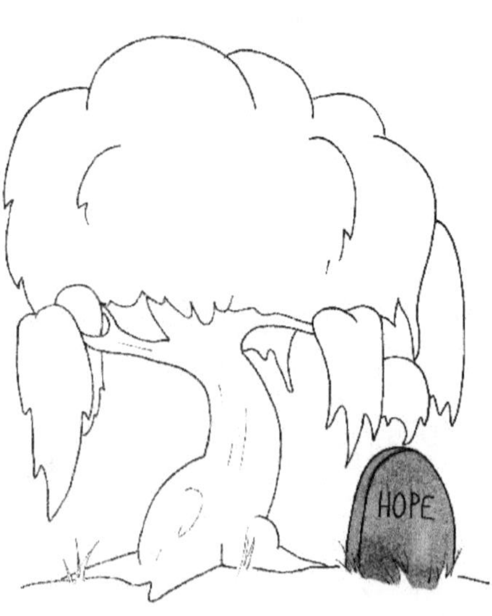

Risk for "Nots"

This not-Spike body,
this not-Buffy body,
not petticoats or lace,
not tall and dark.
Beauty is decay,
not just crushed rose petals
but mushrooms
in the dark and damp.
He walks through maze,
sees his distorted reflections,
does not flinch.
He enjoys it.
Dust shivering off him,
blowing from daylight.
He risked sun
for me.

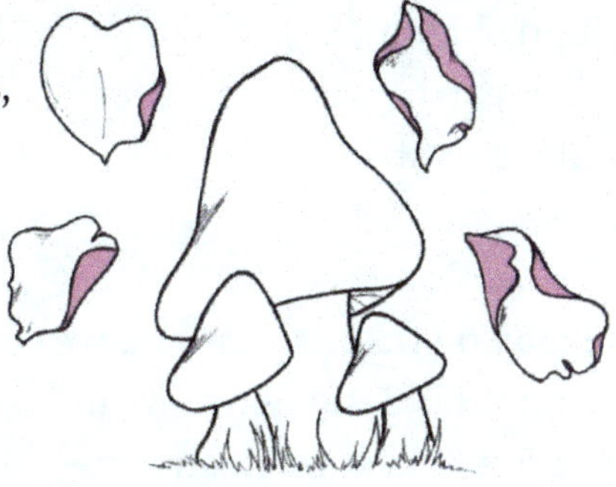

No demon jumps from sunlight
to maze, skin still sizzles
for me.

I Sing into Dark Alleys

"My friends can't face—"

me.

How can one protect themselves
when my lightning strikes?
When I sizzle into their basements
and flounce into their lives
clumsily fierce,
they find shadow
scorched earth,
I am alone in shame.
Cold.

Spike may be trilling that he loves me some dark way
but cannot hold my lightning in his palm
cannot sway chest to electricity
leaves me hollow
alone at threat of ice.

Just spam
telemarketers
and the demon calls to me
with his finger
and in trance, I follow.

Promise with jazz hands no more pet hair,
no more broken dishes,
no more hollow looks.
I overwhelm even my father into silence,

doesn't speak when I enter,
runs from the room.

Lightning does that. Splits trees.
Splits families.
Burns.

The demon tap dances as Spike yells
"No, first I'll kill her—then I'll save her!"

and I wait
      will my friends get to me in time
      or will I dance until I burn?

Magic Multiplied

The mirror
of mirror
of mirror
perplexes
prisms
prisons
and the bad poet me

drained
to pretense.
Plays pretend.
I cannot explain
phoenix
demon to ash
ash in wind
I taste love's metallic
cold prayer
still stuck.

Shadow

His chest flexes,
he is flesh?
My hair parts from neck
tingle and prickle
and go away
and come closer
and I want his bite.
He recoils.
Some stench?
Someone else in labyrinth?
His eye close,
his fangs to neck,
let him bite.
"Slayer, this isn't over."

Call Me The Slayer?

He had looked at my
demon.
And still, called me slayer.
Only way was forward,
past cracking mirrors,
to dusty one, webbed.
Is this me?
Like some orphan bird.
Is this me?
Like shots fired,
I stare, capture the scene.
Would my ashes be painful?
Is "alone" pain?
Loneliness forever?
Body changing to never good enough.
To self-changing to never good enough.
Would love help? Save?

Does it come in the shape of a mirror or stake?
A knife or a party dress?
Is it in my eyes or my embrace?

When Lightnings Collide

Such lightning in belly
thunders shoulders
murky airtight
smog presses deep into pores.
Lights flicker like pulse.
Tension unavoidable
destruction held at my
chest—what if I am,
am the demon ready
to strike? The rhythm
smothers and
oxygen bleeds away
to him.

Of course, mirrors
some fun house game
some hell and
a good deal of steam
I sweat—
take off my not
Buffy jacket.
Hold fast to my
weapon.
And I will dance,
and steam,
glance at internal
storm.
Let the demons
have me—

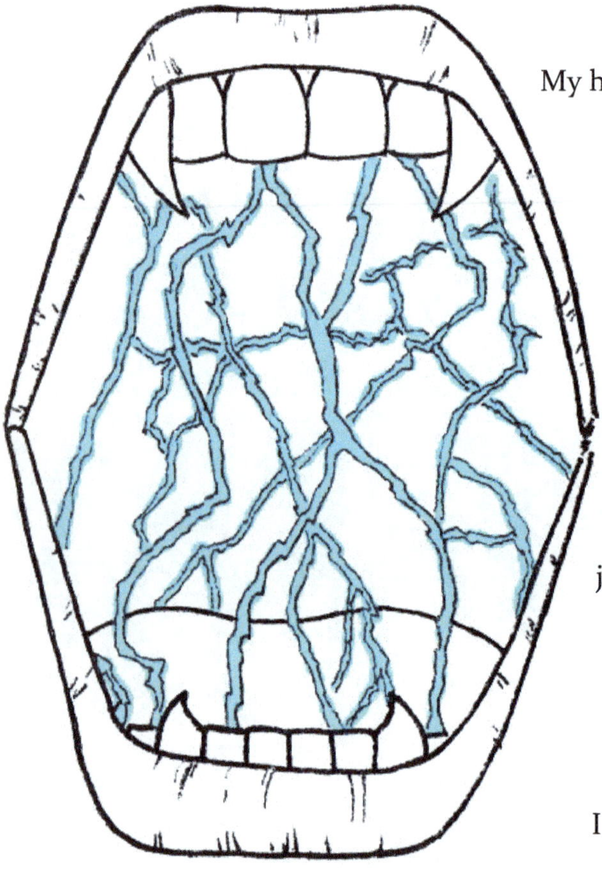

my heart calls me back
to become one of
them.
His eyes are my lightning
the thunder between
his lips ready to
crash my breast
and give me back
my soul.
My hands cinch themselves
beg tight embrace
cannot tempt them
into flesh and his
own demon's beat.
Cropped hair—
blaring face—
tortured—waits for
me.
My demon repels
his—soft—then blows
in belly
jelly soft his hand finds
my waist, thumb
on hip.
I could be his.
For a time.
He was Buffy's.
I do not wear her jeans,
her ass,
but still—his eyes
surrender me.

Switch of the Boot

Unable to look at
own imperfections
I want to say
Please
catches in throat
our demons
dance—some chaotic
caterwauler and baggage
bonded into daydream
paraphernalia
and somehow
after,

I wear Buffy's boots.

First, there must be selflove

echoes like selflove
comes like a spell
rather than jealous
lover waiting for
your time given
in anger, haste,
your reflection,
mine,
crashing in mirror
true, dark circles
smudged brow
and last night's dinner
clinging
to chest.
This mirror cannot lie.
No hell dimension
is loved and martyred
and being unsuspecting victim.
Self-sabotage, emaciation,
blink of vitamins.
Too late for second chances.
Only forward cracks
heart
Love will come next
—in a hell dimension
you just see yourself
in love,
body
numb.

Triage

He knows I hurt
asks where.
I cannot let
him rip out
the hollow
in my chest,
let him slide his fingers
into chasm
burial chamber.
He traces my face,
almost brusk hand
on arm.
Hurt is a word
we both know.
I cannot open,
my soul jump starts.
He whispers,
doesn't say the word 'love'
and I cannot utter 'truth.'

"Impractical" the New Buzz Word

In that not-blonde hair,
in that not-halter top,
in those impractical
boots
I slay.

Hum.

He is gone.
She is gone.
Will the shadows
grace me quiet?
Already, the heat
turned up
solo serenades
staccato improvisation.

There are tears
and shadow outlined, eyes
smoky—beg not
and plastered against
wall.
Mirror. Mirror. Shows
me tall. Buffy bondage
boot leather me not
jacket smooth.
I am toughened.
My hips hard.

Thighs muscle deep
and I could dance
or dig myself
resounding grave.

It isn't like me to
not be
It isn't like me to be
stuck, somehow
sitting mirrored
wall staring into
teacup, porcelain
refined white paste,
watching my lips tremble
treble tea knows
fragility,
knows meditation blistered
tongue,
holds bliss
in pain
truth is
I wait for him,
her, some shovel tongue
some smoke tang
and I want my demon
to breathe before dust
and smoky sunlight.

Age Haunts the Mirror

The mirror I crawled to showed
old, hunched woman.
Bent, smiling shuffling,
no stake.
Only a bunchy leather purse.
Holding flowers.
Edged slowly down three steps—
fading, reshaping to grave.
Some name ached me hollow.
Some name I did not know,
still ash on my tongue.
There are two reflections
in the mirror of mirrors
even the slice of reflection
slammed on floor
tut tut tuts
two blushed faces.
Hand on nape
neck gentled
waist gripped solid
I want the fire back.
I want you to melt soft
breathe hush in ear
unthaw me free.
My eyes dagger
love me. don't love me.
Just stay.

"There's a traitor here beneath my breast"

—Spike "Once More with Feeling"

My body holds tight promise,
understands gamble as possibility,
knows only my love is love—
yours is yours
all ash.
When your hands wrapped me
somehow no icy burn and flinching.
I need your hand on shoulder,
your whisper in my ear.
But the grave whispers instead.
Not real. Not real.
And if our mouths ever meet—
I would not understand dampness
of not love.
Soul connected then disconnected then connected
and stake penetrates deep every time
someone dares to say your name.

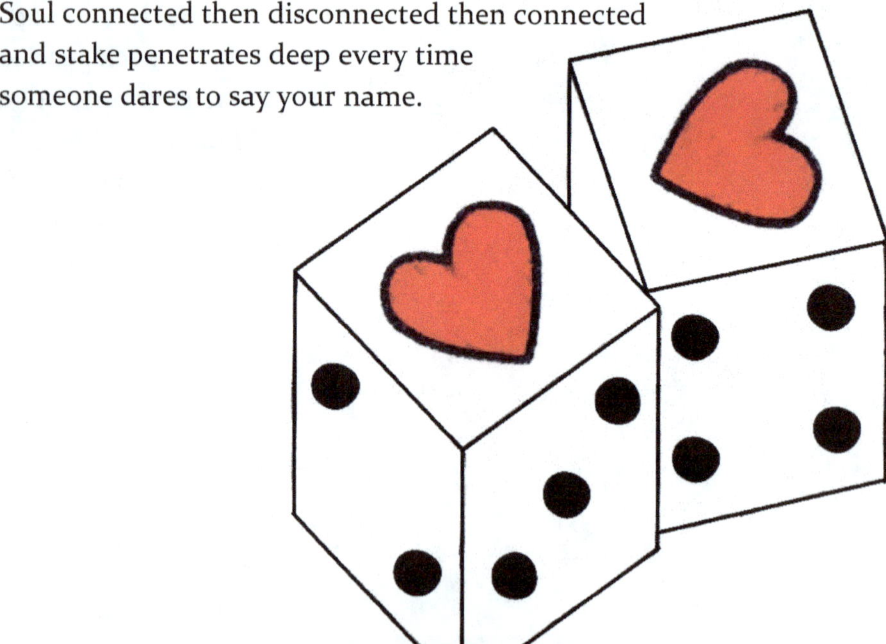

Aged Offering

I stay with the old woman, plump, ancient.
Watch her clean grave,
tend leaves,
take dirt.
Protection.
Vampires roamed
but let her be.
Aura so strong
could she be me—
that not-perfect woman?
Untamed beauty, wild.

Was she activated or just watcher?
This woman knew dangers of dusk,
and still laid down offers of sweet rolls
and blood.
Her basket held wood,
like a sharpened spoon.
Grief.
Combined with old grief.
Betrayal of high school mathematical origami,
a knife in her belly.
Scent of sweet rolls
even as the shadow pressed deep into her
Evil slid by First,
the wind panted her breathworn.

A Not Perfect Slayer?

Buffy feared? Buffy pained?
Buffy Dead? Resurrected?
Buffy shallow love
with love right
and love wrong
and scars
and demons.
She could hold close
betrayal, be the big bad,
age, love monster,
slay evil,
love someone no different than Spike.
Because she did not drink,
she did not feed.

I Stumble into Blue

Soaked in too much sunlight.
Sizzle.
Even if grave swallows me
I would overfill it
take more than what I deserve
more than what is mine.
Thick blue flashes in the distance,
overtop of me.
Then, darkness.
I saw him
jaw tight.
Perfectly tangled,
with deadly drawl.
Am I at war with him
or my mouth?
Gasping at his temper,
fiery love.
He takes up space.
Unafraid.
I want fangs and glimmer,
hand gliding me through mirrors
to the right
one
to the right me.

Redefined Definitions

Smolder
is defined
by breast
and heat
deep gasps
blush.
He glistens
sweat and steam
sunlight succulent
and he is here for me.
She pounds from within
chest locked tight.
I cock my hips. Pretend bold.
Wait for shimmering speech.

I Do Not Need

demon.
Could stamp her free.
Execute her.
My shadow swift to ash.
It will happen somewhen
anyway.
I cannot say how
ice blue became velvet
deep cherry
to orange liquor
marmalade plunged
into plum.
On a tilted path
up and down.
I had no lust.
I had anger.
Left.
Made without bite.
Bondaged at birth to loathe
every inch of flesh,
every pound of soul.

Not Today

He glowered.
Orange light jumping
into brow
leaping off
dizzy
and I must have held shadow
and scorn
and vacillated
my tongue rhythmic
and strong.
Luscious, untouchable.
Unwilling to hand myself
to a step right up, step right up
wo/man
with bills and sexy hands.
I could have.
Might have.
Even with my demon
that begged to crawl to them
to blister
for blood and family.

If I Could

Did I learn defense against myself?
I would bear the cuts,
if I could love my scars.
I do not need the vampire
waiting to love into my neck,
take me into soulless frenzy.
I am not all demon.
I do not know if my soul exists.
My hips are my hips.
My tongue my tongue.
I need no definition,
no protection
against me
     against him
         against her
            against
                 her
            demons
        and his
     demon
soulless
     and the scared
         the scarred
            the love does not
               need
            innuendo
        to matter
     to save
me.

Resuscitation Rhythm

My heart is slave
in chest, blood
leaked out.
Tongue licks my neck
and I bite
back
sink into wrist
faint murmur of the man
seeking me
in the not mirror.

Mouth to mouth
resuscitation might be
nice with peroxide
and purple light
less heated
less needed.
This demon—
slayed?

Could it be—
    tamed?
Could marmalade
blush sweet?
Could toast crisp
at her teeth?

I shuddered
taste.
Love was his hand.
The not vampire hand
telling her loud—
    (not angry)
      "Eat."
Here in the mirror
I saw her stiff back
her disbelieving.
My face.
My gasp.
No betrayal.
The vampire sidesteps
and he places hand on
chest.
Heart skips
a beat
wrong
but not
still
not dead yet.

Cannot Cannot Trust the Splinter

Heart not beating
                    mouth open no
                                resuscitation needed
                                cannot cannot trust
mirror image
                    cheekbone love
                                        palms flexed
cramping and eyes
        creep hopeful
                dagger downward
                        not enough
                                        cannot let go
                            cannot cannot fall into
                                mirror life
cannot fall backwards
        into waiting arms
                reflecting mirror
                        trust is handing the stake
                            over to the Slayer herself
baring chest
        hoping for the bite
                and splinter.
Pain beneath
skin creeps
they cannot
remove me with knife
or tweezer
or bloody needle and spit.
                    I am splintered.

Cannot free myself
encased in my own
snare drum recipe.

Their not love
    and their faux love
        and I get under their skin
            trapped.

Could I slide out of mirror
house, tilted floors untilt,
    and could I save myself
    from splintered syncopation
    of the stake?

Bait Permitted

The vampire came near.
Anger left,
pointed at the flowered mirror
stupid bit
           is love is love is love?
Love defined different
permission given until
I could allow or skewer myself
my demon chip her
and hold deep.
The vampire leered,
brushed nape
about to kiss
my unchipped
self my melodious
insecurity, misunderstanding
power of without.
Of no sacrifice.
No solitude.
No need for flings.

Battle Scarred Permission

Fangs at collar bone
pressed tight and tight
and warm
and this was love
and this was not love
and not love and not love
unwanted.
I felt her sing in
my breast.
No need. No begging. Was not love
worth more?
No. No love was better than weakness
and pain.

Baited Becoming

I saw him come
from over shoulder.
Stake in hand.
Grimacing, I was sacrifice.
I took my weapon before he

lifted his and my vampire
      shadowed to dust.
I fell, weak.
So strong. So strong.
     So strong.

He holds a stake
could destroy what was inside
could quench
my worst
desire
to have
Buffy beauty, Buffy strength.
I get Spike's, whimsy and
freneticism, sarcastic randy,
and I had my
trunk, my pose,
and my goddamn stake.

I held thunder

in my hips,
shoulders—lightning.
My demon quiet
in his presence.
These mirrors do not
show the future.
The mouth that places
death and kisses heart
but takes away
cookies and carrots,
his eyes hold no judgement
of failure after failure
and I stand
face failure
demon
again and again
search out food
as penance
cannot taste pleasure
in it like one with fangs.

Battle Hardened

I do not need Buffy.
I am the slayer.
I slay others' demons
and mine,
I hold close,
waiting for her to strike.

The Calvary Comes

He comes as friend
as gesture ready
to fight me
to save me from me
and my heart still
beats
my collar bleeds
We do not
live song
live ourselves
perseverance, acceptance,
beat those demons
down
send them skyward
brush their ash into
elms
but I sing offkey
not because of demon lord
or spell.
I did taste heaven,
taste sometimes enough.
I permit myself.
I fight myself.
The funhouse bids
me slay fast.
But love is slow
to come,
acceptance
is slow to come.

The Mirror Is No Demon

My cellulite shame
thin hair
pockmarked skin
dimples I don't like
my damn feet
those scared toes

and he awes at insecurity
shakes head with laugh
no, no it does not matter.

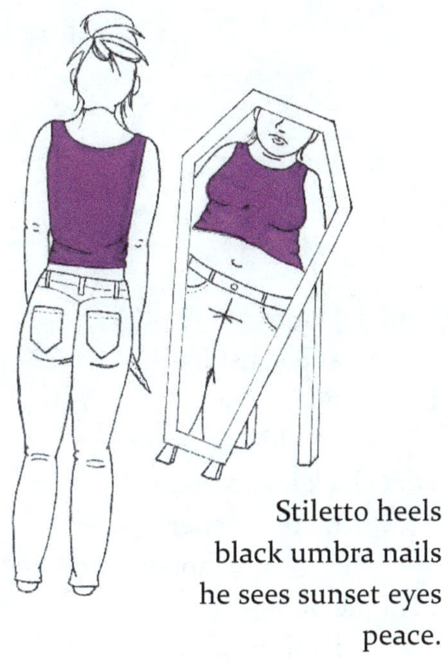

Stiletto heels
black umbra nails
he sees sunset eyes
peace.

Mirror. Scale. Beat
them. Crack them.
Dream them far.
Let them fall off your cliff
Banish them to some Hell
dimension.

I want to banish,
plead.

up.

I hold myself

Allowed to be seen,
     take up space,
          arms wide,
               legs spread,
                    not hunched inward
                         breathing
                              scared.

                              She does not claw
                                   and bite.

I am my hair
     and sunshine.
I am bondage boots
     and black leather.
I am cloak and corset.
     Letter opener dagger
          strapped into bun.
I am the old me.
     I am the older me.
          The last me that had weight.
I am grit.
I am taste of honey,
blood red wine,
     scream into sunset
for more
adventures
more companionship
more smiles
     and that is love.

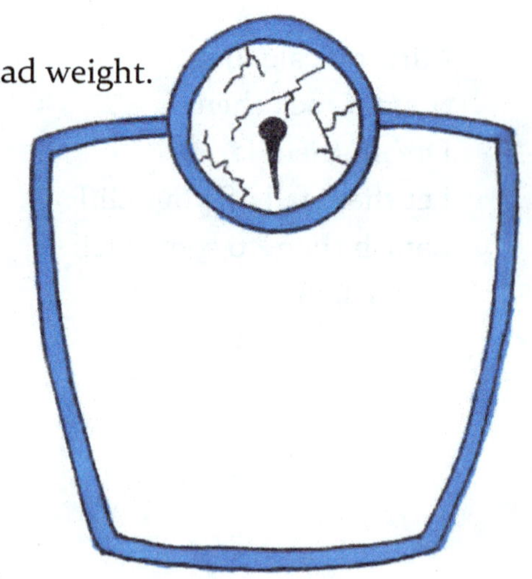

Mirror. Scale. Beat them. Crack them.

This is the mirror that is me.

Glue and Time and Duct Tape

No one told me mirrors
crack.
You might too
but there is time to piece yourself
together.
Glue and time and duct tape.
You might shatter again
        remedy
glue and time and duct tape

and love does not
need sweat
        and smooth lips.

Love may be lips
        need only hand
to guide safe while jumping
        cliff to cliff.

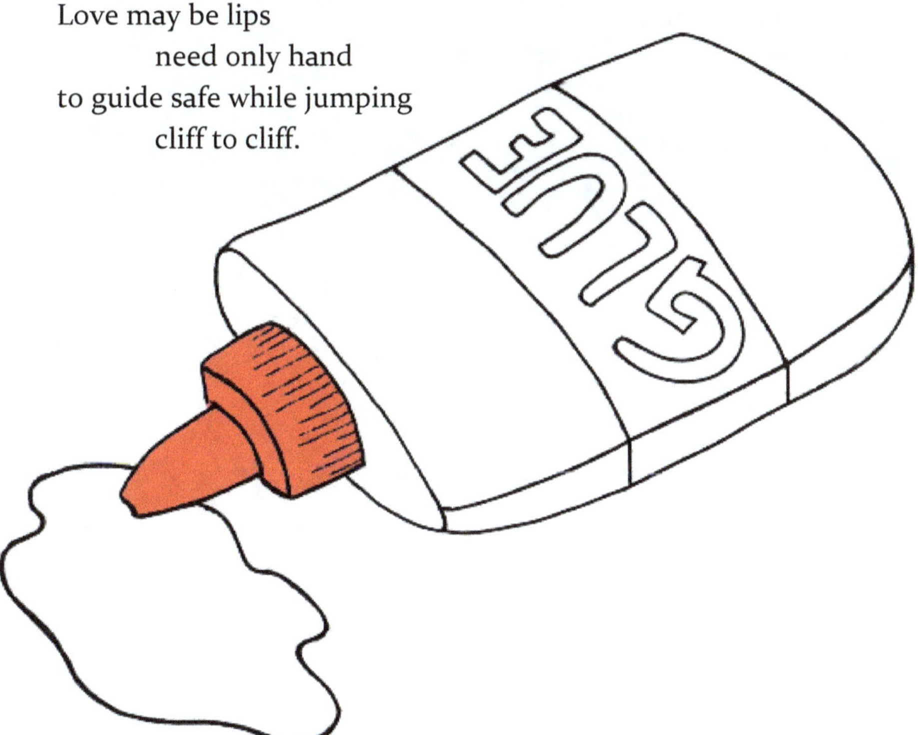

Victims Aren't Victims Forever?

Love burns acid
chains link
but if trees knot themselves
make root village vows
we can bind our needs.
Give each other space to grow
a tug, a boost.

I can root.
He can tangle.
No need for
curtain call kiss.

But if the demon
        not-demon
calls

he will know it bites.

Calvary Reprise

He comes
no stake, hand
outstretched
to save me from maze
guides me past the mirrors.
We are both slayers.
We can fight the other's demon.
I don't take his hand.
I hold my stake.
I grip his.
This is my house of mirrors.

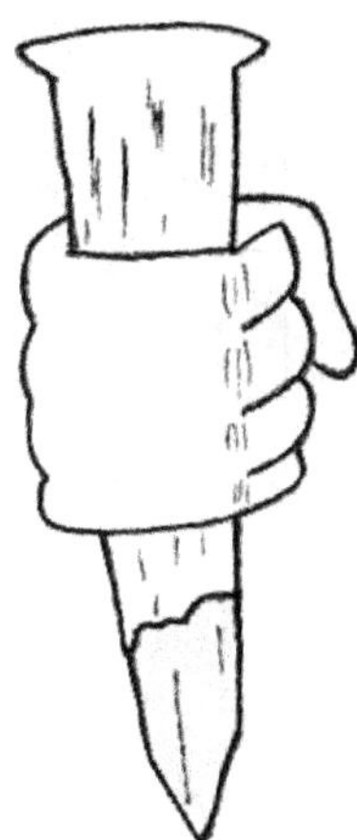
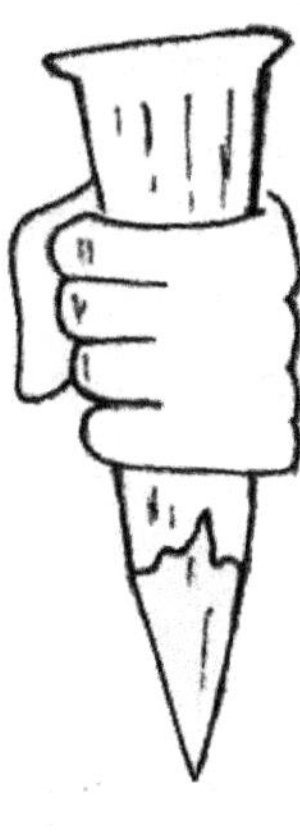

Mirrored Escape

Scarred lips searing.
Arm around me, steel.
Each fun house mirror warbles
not to leave.
I can't prophesy if I keep
walking down that road
of endless mirrors
of endless lies and lives
or if you make a right turn into me
and I stop.
I cannot tell you which crossroads
we place nails in or which ribbons.
Bliss is momentary,
burning is forever.
And the House of Mirrors shatters
with my heel
and you capture me into leather vixen
with stake.
And my Spike holds me in the sun
without smoldering.

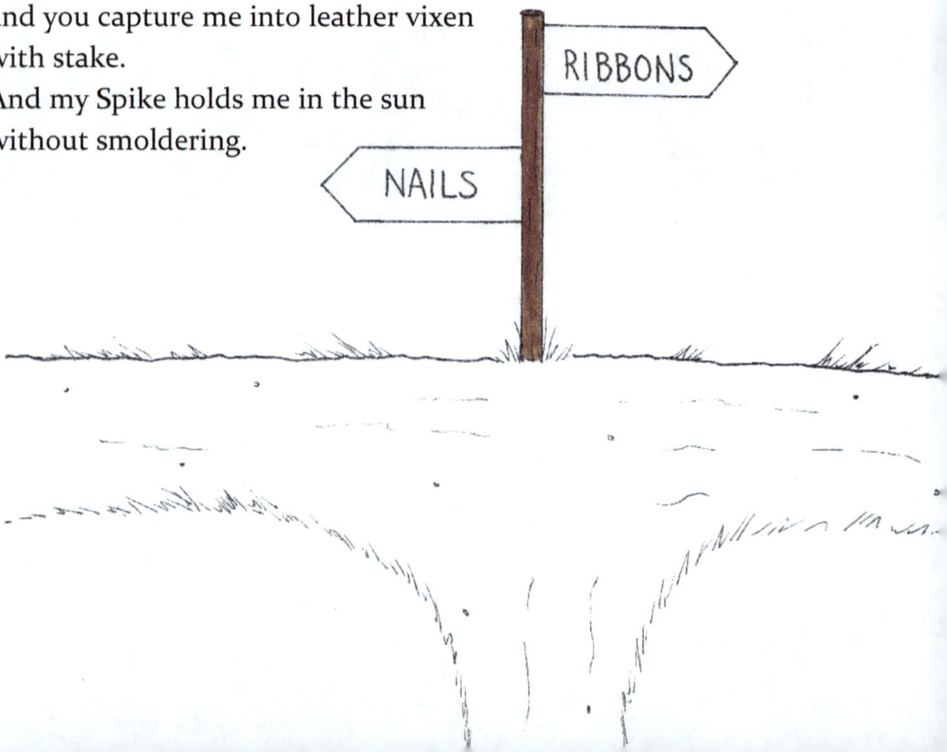

Curtain Call Kiss

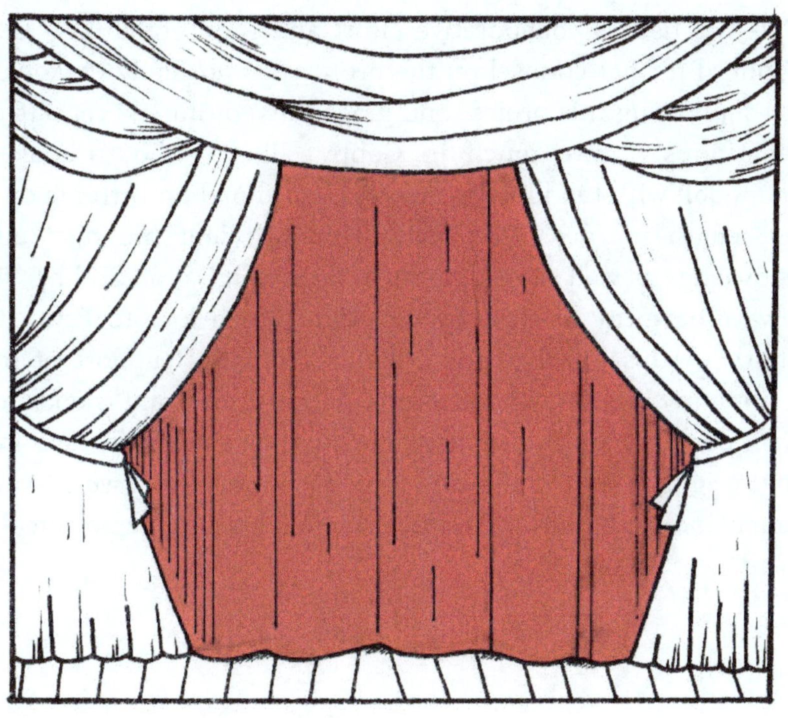

The End

Thanks

This has been a collaborative effort and I am grateful to Kate Wolford for her counsel on the prototype and Emily Perkovich for supporting this project and gracefully editing my repeats of repetitions. I owe much to Gabby Gilliam who to took a chapbook with ten illustrations and continued on with me on a full-length journey. Ty Chadwell-English lent me his Buffy knowledge as well as reading my rough, rough draft and he will always have my deepest appreciation. Much love to Bryan C. Smith for his photography and his continual support of my writing my journey. Thank you to all my family and friends for their constant joy and support. Finally, I owe the Buffy fans and the originators for allowing me to share their world and reimagine our bodies and reimagine what love our demons really need.

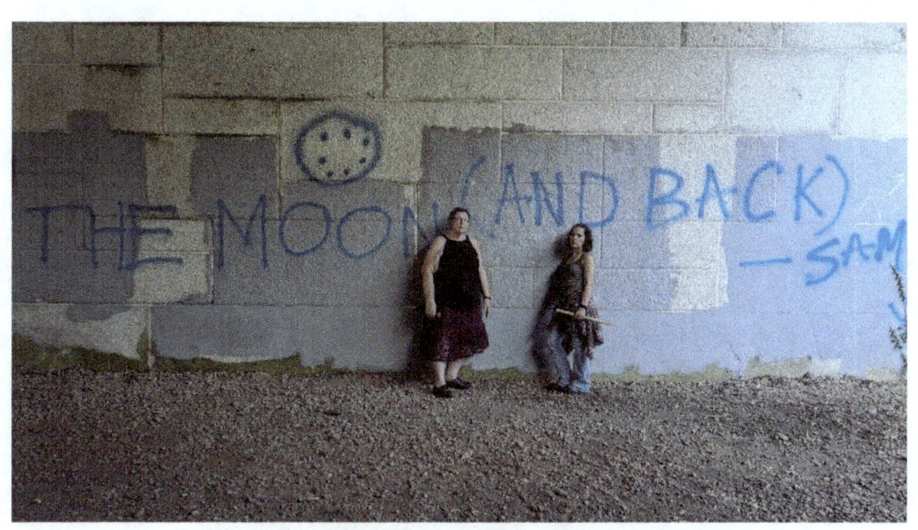
THE MOON (AND BACK)
—SAM

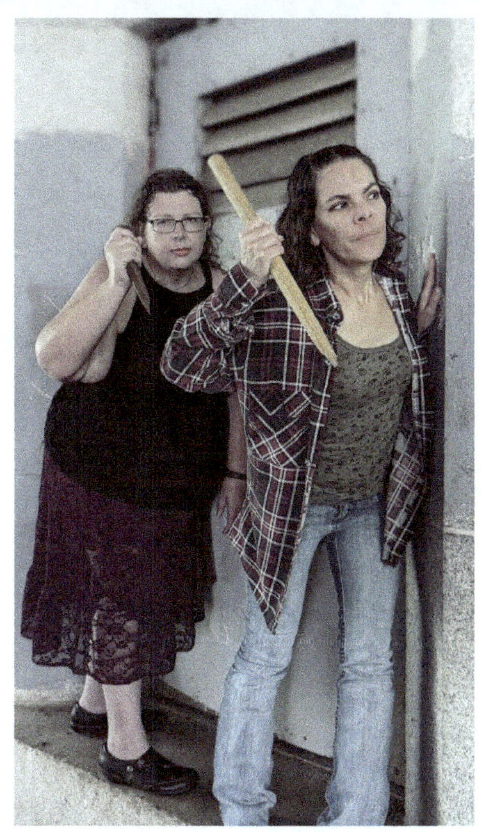